This book
belongs to:

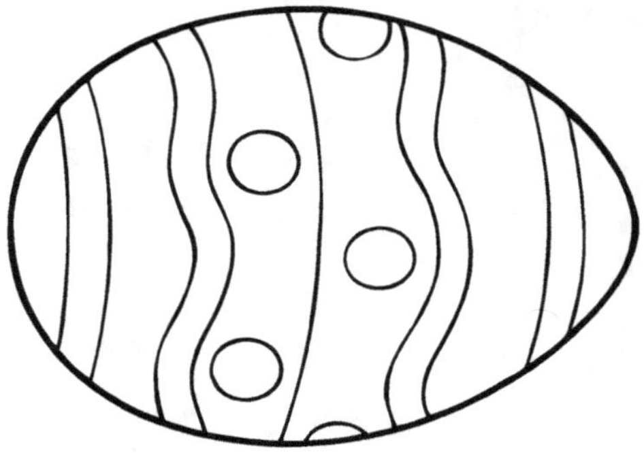

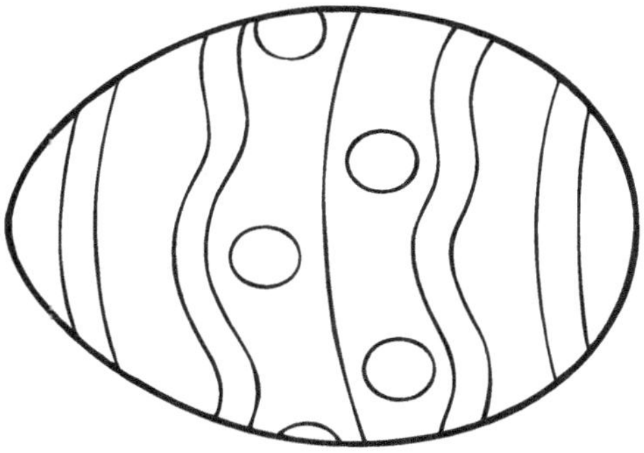

Funny Bunny & Friends

Coloring Book

Sandy Mahony
Mary Lou Brown

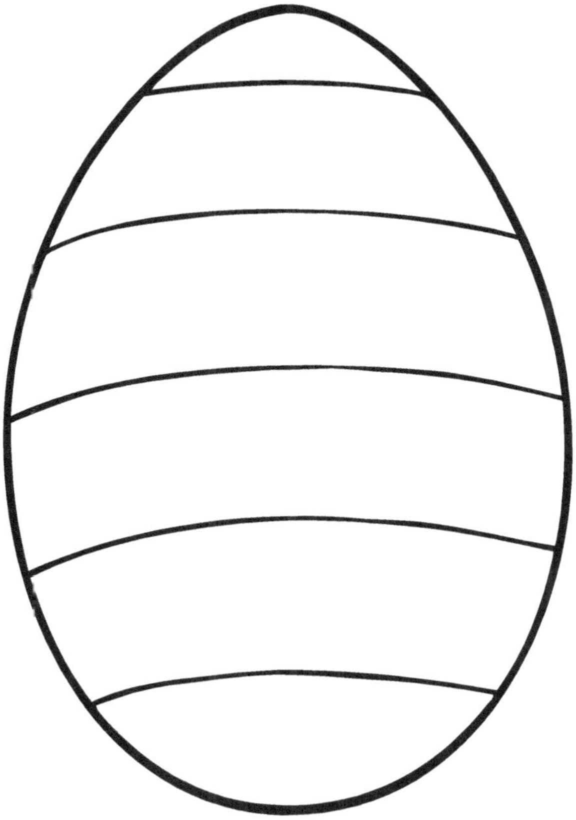

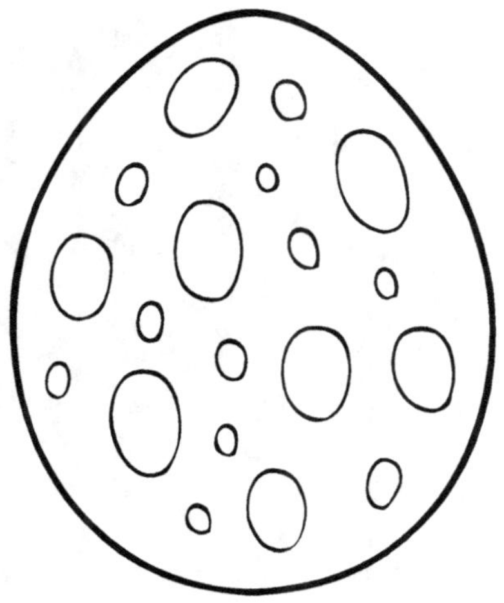

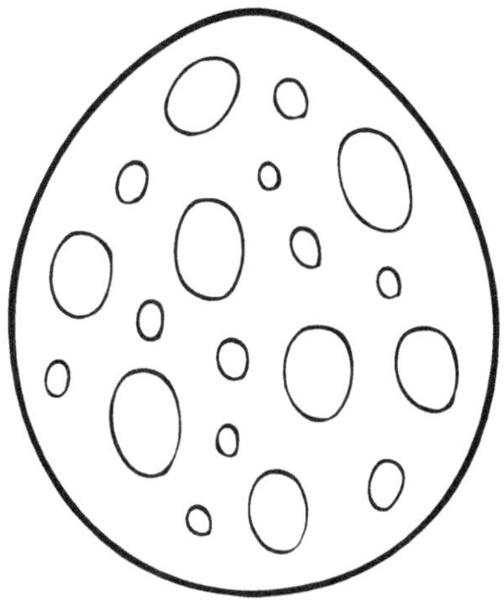

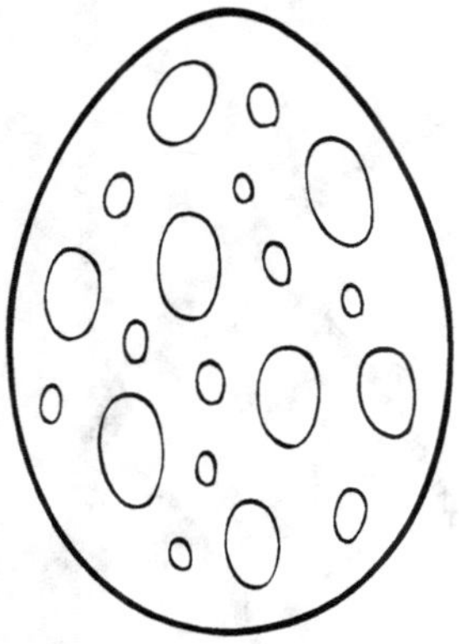

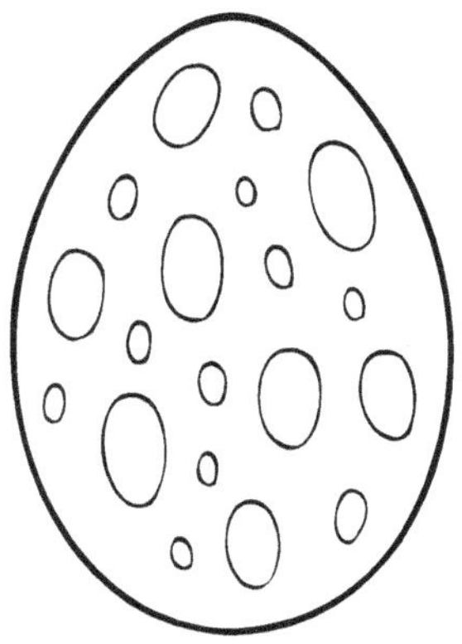

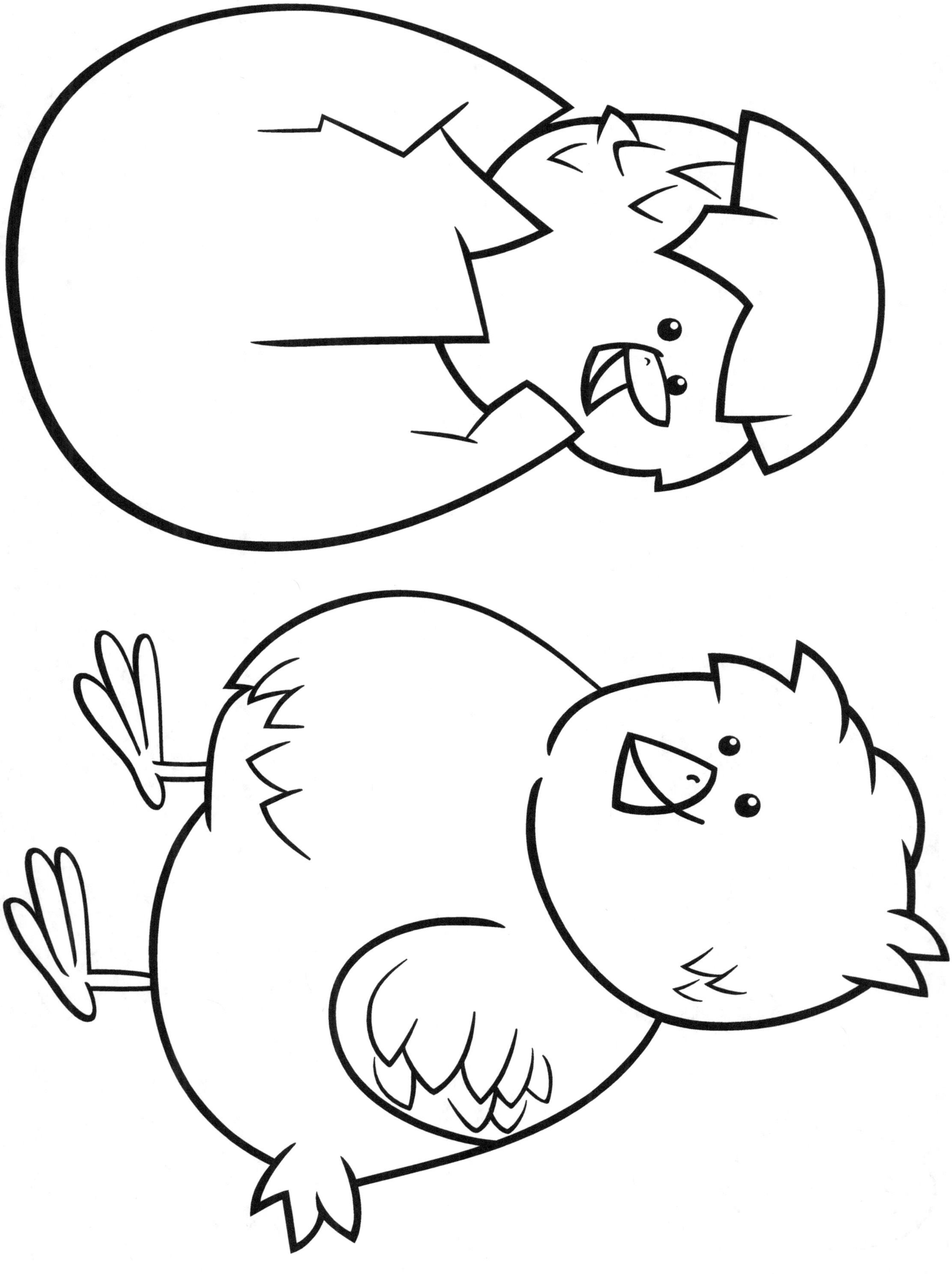

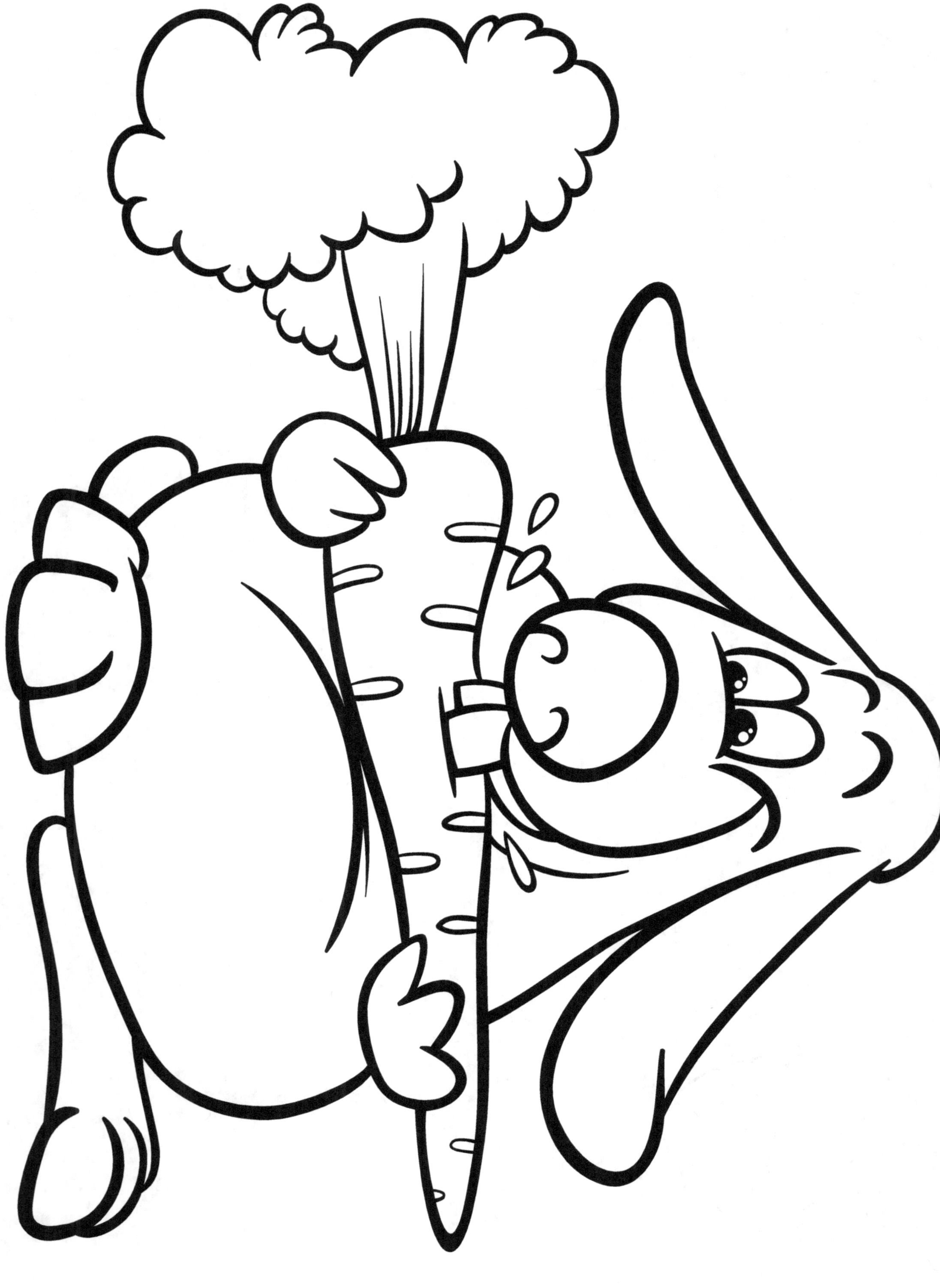

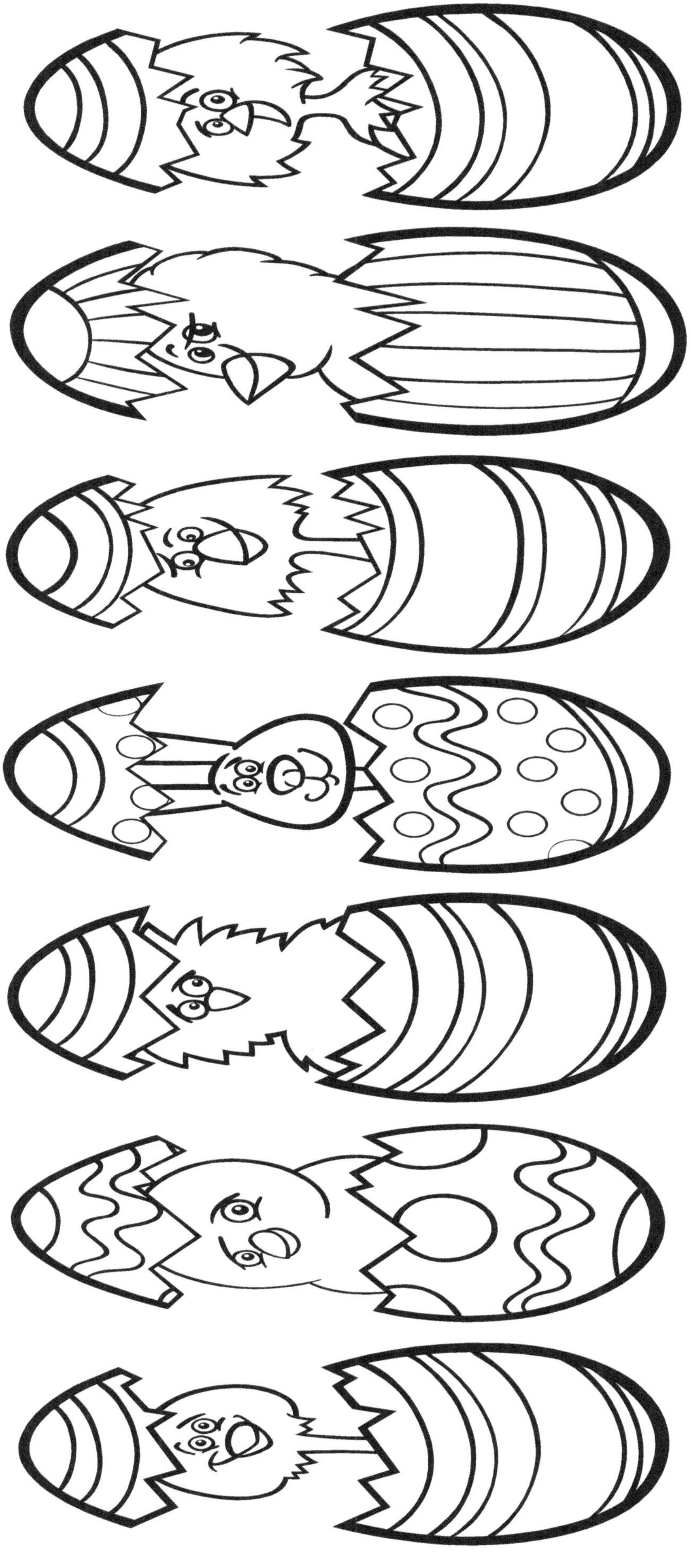

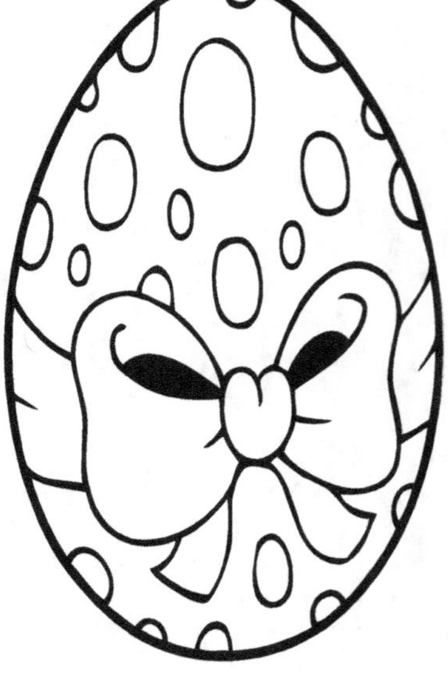

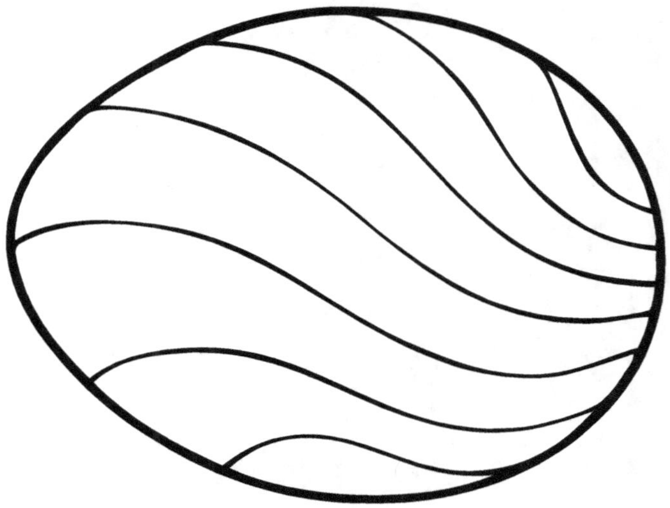

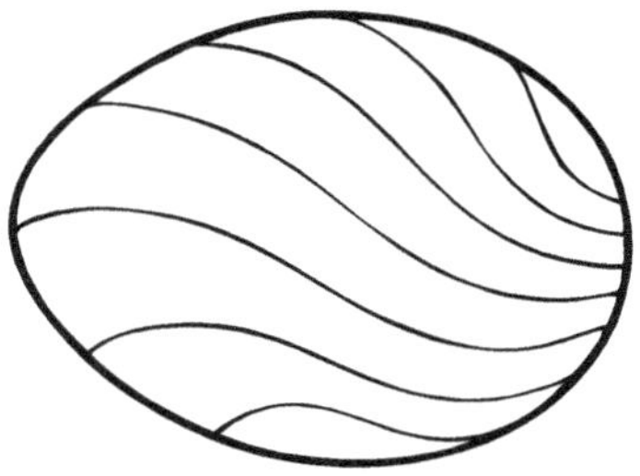

adventurelearningpress.com

www.ingramcontent.com/pod-product-compliance
Lightning Source LLC
Chambersburg PA
CBHW081416280526
45788CB00009B/3130